INSTALLING

Ubuntu Desktop 23.04

AUTHORS

AHMED NOOR KADER MUSTAJIR MD EUSOFF
MUHAMMAD ASYRAF WAHI ANUAR

EDITORS

MOHD ZAILAN ENDIN
AZMI AB RAHMAN

Printed in the United States of America

Preface

This book provides guidance on how to install Ubuntu Desktop 23.04 (Lunar Lobster) on the computer. Ubuntu is one of the popular distributions or distro Debian Linux based operating systems. Included in book are the screenshot of the screen to guide in steps installing Ubuntu in simple approach.

As the Ubuntu Desktop 23.04 has the latest installer application with the legacy installer, both cover in this book. The latest installer is based on flutter apps and legacy installer provided there as alternatives for the user to choose. With the screenshot included for both installers, hopefully can help with a much effective step by step process.

Hopefully this book can help in guiding installing Ubuntu Desktop 23.04 and enjoy Linux as operating systems.

Disclaimer

In the book, included simple steps in installing Ubuntu Desktop 23.04. The guide included the hyperlink to download the Ubuntu Desktop 23.04. Brief explanation regarding Ubuntu Desktop 23.04.

Installation Ubuntu 23.04 may install directly to the computer as owner wants or use any virtualization software like VirtualBox, VMware and others virtualization software.
The screenshot of the installation process is based on the installation done on VirtualBox. Installation was done on VirtualBox simple as enable better view and can be repeated so the screenshot is better.

Screenshots in the book were done by the author and not taken from any other online sources. This is to avoid copyright infringement issues with the respective owners. Ubuntu website screenshots were made to show the website and show the source of download installer.

Font use in this book is using Ubuntu Font Family which can be downloaded free from *https://design.ubuntu.com/font*. Ubuntu Font Family can used in your computer and by default its already install in Ubuntu Desktop.

Contents

GETTING UBUNTU 23.04

Getting Ubuntu

Ubuntu is downloadable from the official Ubuntu website, ***https:// ubuntu.com.*** The website provides details on Ubuntu and Canonical Ltd. Downloads are available from Ubuntu Desktop, Ubuntu Server, Ubuntu for IoT, and Ubuntu Cloud via four primary submenus. Each is designed to meet the specific requirements of the user. Select the Ubuntu Desktop version for this installation, which includes both the normal release and Long Term Support (LTS).

The primary difference between normal and major releases is that the regular release includes free security and maintenance updates for nine months, whereas the LTS includes free security and maintenance updates for five years. The LTS version is appropriate for production machine users who require a stable feature application, whereas the regular release will contain the most recent application and features.

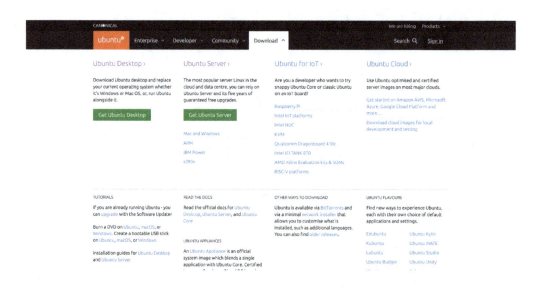

From the download page, choose the Ubuntu Desktop by clicking

Get Ubuntu Desktop

There will be two versions of the release of Ubuntu, the LTS and regular release. For this installation, choose the regular release not the LTS release. Also, the availability of the system requirement and version release notes in the same page.

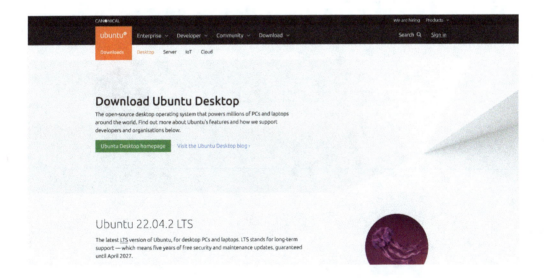

This shows the Ubuntu LTS and the system requirement. This page provides additional link and information.

The latest LTS release were Ubuntu LTS 22.04 LTS which provide five years of free security and maintenance updates, guaranteed until April 2027.

Ubuntu 22.04.2 LTS

The latest LTS version of Ubuntu, for desktop PCs and laptops. LTS stands for long-term support — which means five years of free security and maintenance updates, guaranteed until April 2027.

Ubuntu 22.04 LTS release notes

Recommended system requirements:

- 2 GHz dual-core processor or better
- 4 GB system memory
- 25 GB of free hard drive space
- Internet access is helpful
- Either a DVD drive or a USB port for the installer media

Download 22.04.2

For other versions of Ubuntu Desktop including torrents, the network installer, a list of local mirrors and past releases see our alternative downloads.

Ubuntu 23.04

The latest version of the Ubuntu operating system for desktop PCs and laptops, Ubuntu 23.04 comes with nine months of security and maintenance updates, until January 2024.

Recommended system requirements are the same as for Ubuntu 22.04 LTS.

Ubuntu 23.04 release notes

Scroll down, then will see the latest regular release which Ubuntu 23.04 Lunar Lobster which the current release. This release will support nine months of security and maintenance updates, until January 2024.

Lunar Lobster is the codename for the Ubuntu 23.04 release.

Clicking the download button, *Download 23.04*, also have the alternative download, *Download 23.04 (Legacy Desktop Installer).*

The latest installer using Flutter apps backed by subiquity and packaged as a snap while the legacy installer is still available in case of issues with the new installer.

This installation will cover both the latest installer and legacy installer.

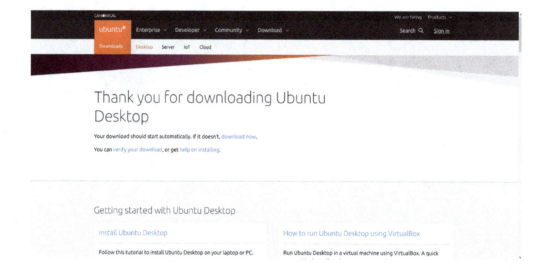

Bottom of the download page, also provided additional link for extra reading and guidance.

You can verify your download, or get help on installing.

Getting started with Ubuntu Desktop

Install Ubuntu Desktop

Follow this tutorial to install Ubuntu Desktop on your laptop or PC.
You can also run Ubuntu from a USB to try it without installing.

How to run Ubuntu Desktop using VirtualBox

Run Ubuntu Desktop in a virtual machine using VirtualBox. A quick
start guide that will work across any operating system.

How to install Ubuntu Desktop on Raspberry Pi 4

A complete guide to installing Ubuntu Desktop on a Raspberry Pi 4
(2GB or above).

Upgrade Ubuntu Desktop

If you're already running Ubuntu, you can upgrade in a few clicks from
the Software Updater.

Release notes link provided before contain list of information such as support lifespan, new features, updated packages platforms, Ubuntu flavors, bugs and others.

Release Notes link:

https://discourse.ubuntu.com/t/lunar-lobster-release-notes/31910

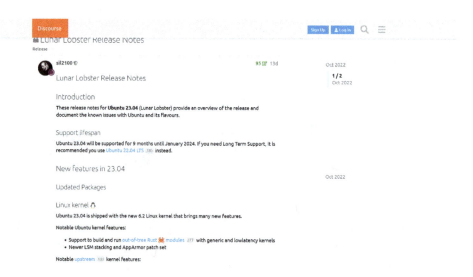

After having downloaded the ISO file, may burn the ISO to the DVD or USB flash drive if want to install directly to the computer or can use virtualization software like VirtualBox to install Ubuntu in the virtualization environment.

For this installation, will be using the VirtualBox for the Ubuntu Desktop installation and all the steps showing are the result of print screen of the VirtualBox application.

Ubuntu Install

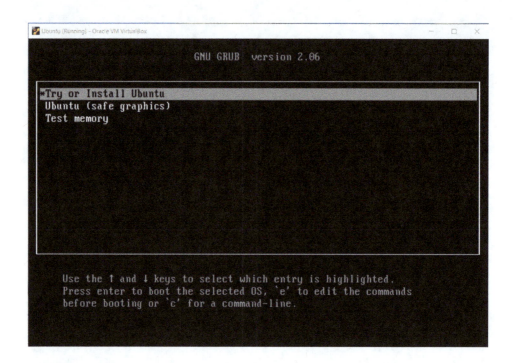

Choose menu

Try or Install Ubuntu

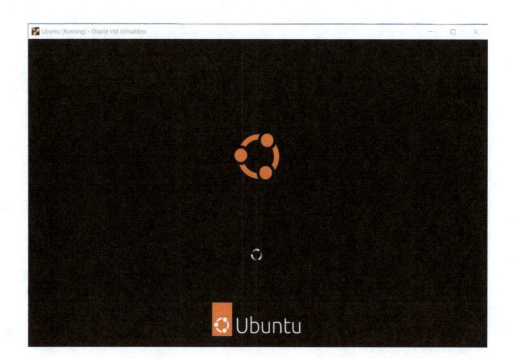

Ubuntu will be loaded into the memory of the computer. This process will take time depending of the hardware of the computer.

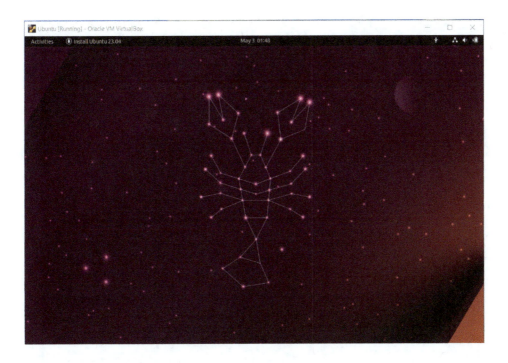

The Graphical User Interface (GUI) of Ubuntu 23.04 is based on Gnome version 44 code name "Kuala Lumpur". For information about Gnome 44, https://release.gnome.org/44/

A Windows will pop up, and this is the starting point of installation process. Wait until all the content in the Windows appears.

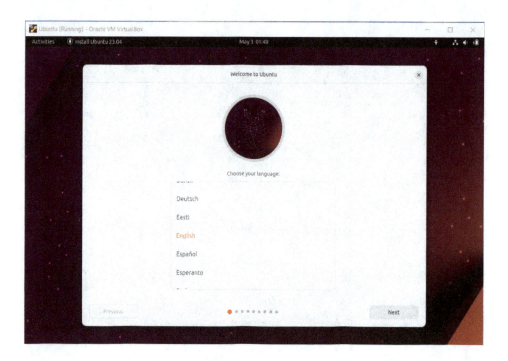

Choose the language want to use during the installation process.

Two option available, *Install Ubuntu* which will install Ubuntu into the computer and *Try Ubuntu* where can play around with Ubuntu without needing to install.

Select *Install Ubuntu* the click *Next*

Choose the Keyboard Layout and Keyboard variant as required according to the computer. Can click *Detect* if want automatically selects. Proceed by clicking *Next*.

Connection to Internet useful because will install the extra soft-ware and updated packages during the installation process. Con-nection to the internet can be via wired connection or Wi-Fi.

If have poor connection speed, may choose the option *I don't want to connect to the internet just now*. Then click *Next* to proceed to the next step.

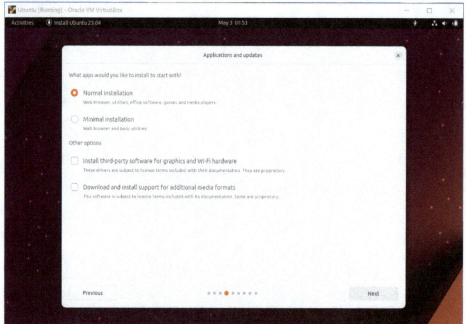

Choose *Normal installation* as install the application recommend-ed by Ubuntu. *Minimal installation* if have storage limitations.

Worry free, as the application can be installed later after installa-tion is completed if required.

Check the options *Install third-party software for graphic and Wi-Fi hardware* as well as *Download and install support for additional media formats* as this helps automatically install additional requirement driver and codecs.

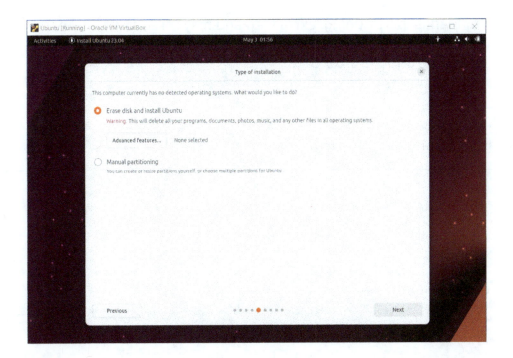

This step will create the required partition, select *Erase disk and Install Ubuntu* as this will automatically create.

For Advance Features, please refer to Advance Features partition on page 37. As the step needs to be taken extra carefully and cannot be undone after that.

For Manual partitioning, extra step and may refer to manual partition on page 41. As the step needs to be taken extra carefully and cannot be undone after that.

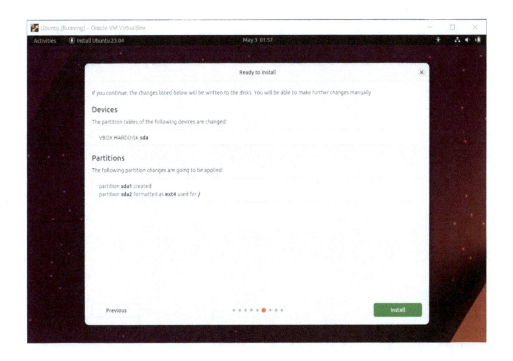

This will be confirmation in creating the partition, confirm with action by click **Install**. If need necessary changes, click **Previous** and make the modification required.

Click on your current location on the maps, the time zone will select automatically. Click **Next** to proceed.

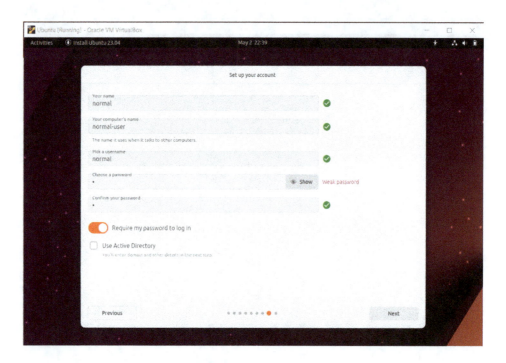

Fill in the information required and make sure to use a strong password to secure the account.

If using a not secure password, notification **Weak Password** will show beside the password field.

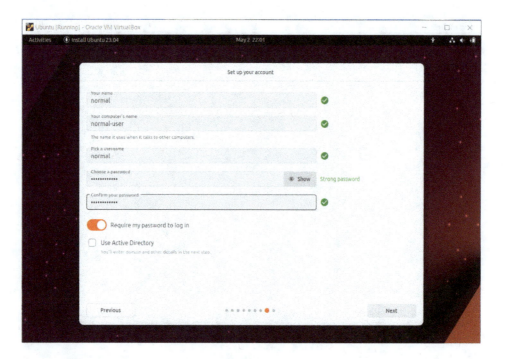

Strong Password notification appears if the password meets the security requirement.

Select the ***Required my password to log*** in to make sure the user log into the system has the right privilege.

For the login **Use Active Directory**, extra step and may refer to on page 47. As the step needs to be taken and verification required.

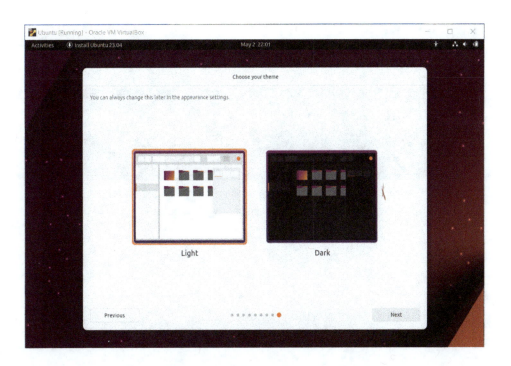

Choose the theme, **Light** Mode or **Dark** mode, the click **Next**.

This screen is the installation process, just leave as it until the process completed.

Screen will change from time to time as the process of installation.

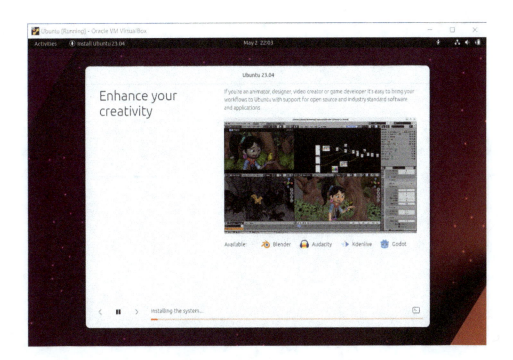

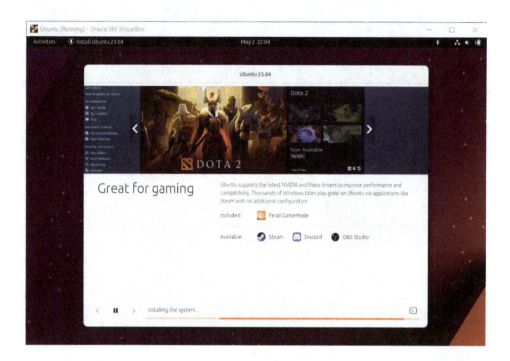

Screen will change from time to time as the process of installation.

Screen will change from time to time as the process of installation.

During the installation, if click item in red, will show the progress of installation.

Showing the progress of the installation.

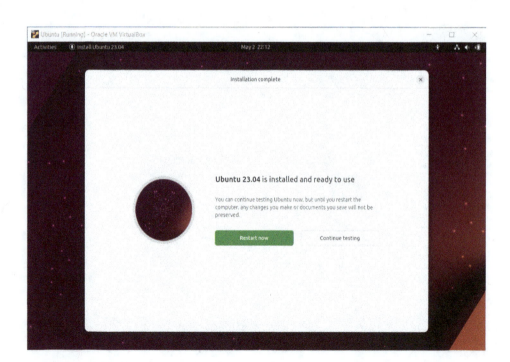

Click **Restart** to complete the installation, or still want to browse the live Ubuntu, click **Continue testing** to explore.

The process restarting in progress.

Remove the installation media. If using DVD or USB flash drive remove the drive, or using ISO unmount the media in the virtualization application.

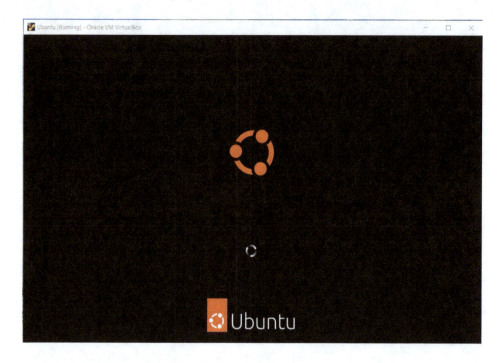

After the media removal, the process rebooting will continue.

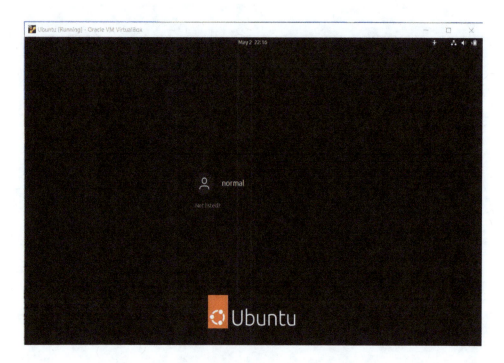

Login Screen will show, and list the username created before and click the username.

Input the password created before.

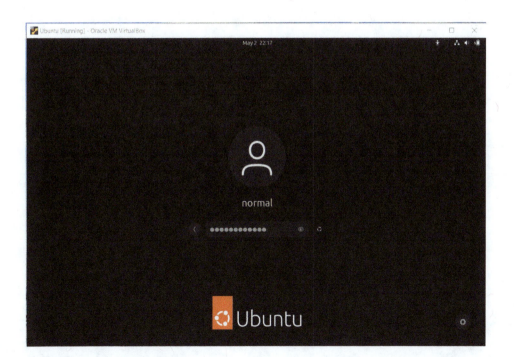

Then click to proceed.

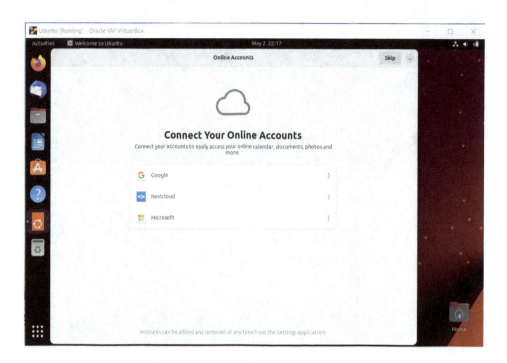

A window will show, to connect to Online Accounts or may proceed by clicking the **Skip** button on top right.

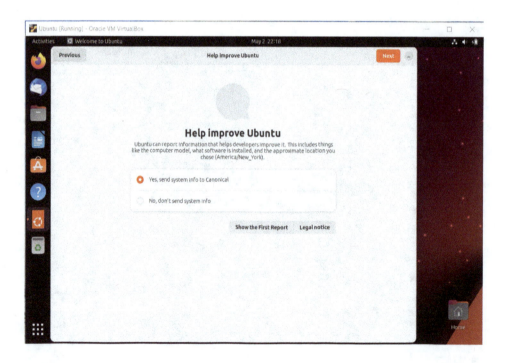

Option to share the information system, if agree to share select **Yes, send system info to Canonical** or disagrees select **No, don't send system info**. Then click **Next** to continue.

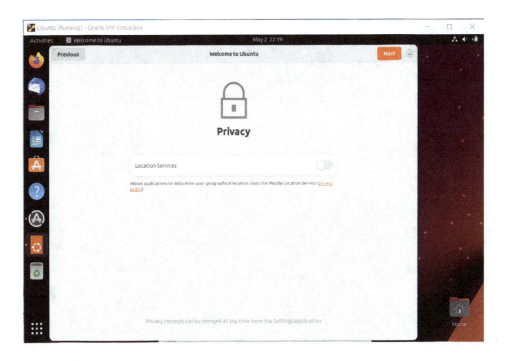

Location Services if enable will help to automatically detect the location of the computer. Click *Next* to proceed to the next step.

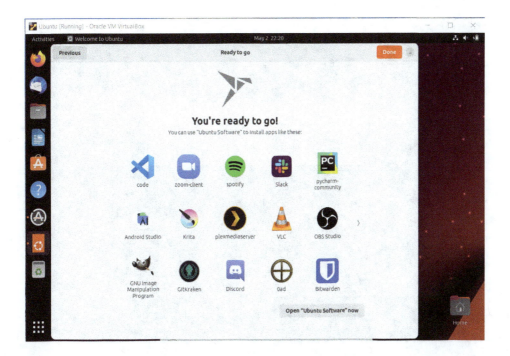

All the primary steps were completed. Click *Done* to end the process and if want to add/remove software may click Open *Ubuntu Software*.

If a new update is available, a window will appear showing the information about the update. Click I**nstall Now** if want to update

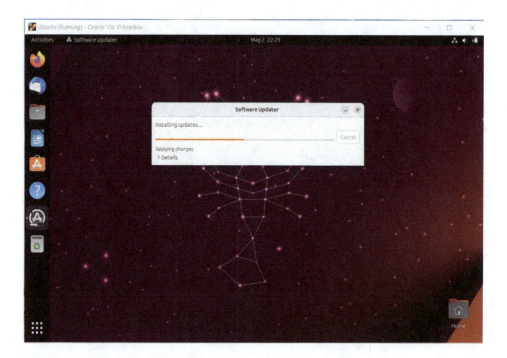

Showing the update progress.

Showing the completed update progress.

For manual update refer page *81*

On bottom left have 9 dots, here will list application available/installed in the Ubuntu.

Type **Setting** in the searching field then click the application link to open it.

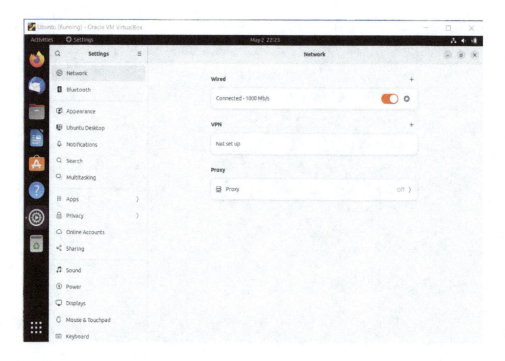

In here, user can modify any setting in the Ubuntu.

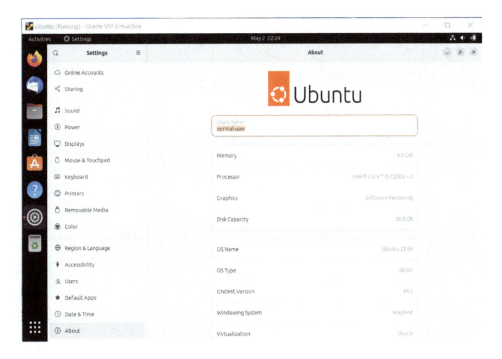

Showing the information about the Ubuntu installation.

ADVANCED FEATURES (PARTITION)

The page will cover the advanced features creating partition for Ubuntu 23.04 and this make extra security and functionality.

For Manual partitioning, extra step and may refer to manual partition on page 41. As the step needs to be taken extra carefully and cannot be undone after that.

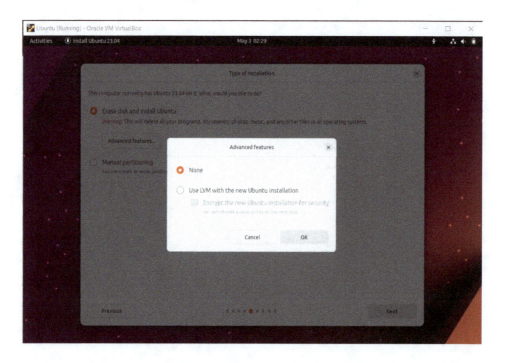

By default, the selection is None.

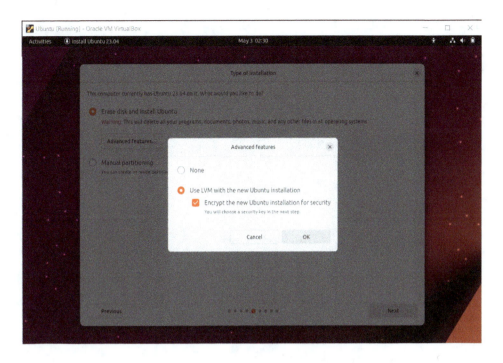

Select *Use LVM with the new Ubuntu Installation* and check also *Encrypt the new Ubuntu installation for security*. Then click *OK* to proceed.

After completing, on Advanced features will be shown *LVM and encryption selected*. Then click *Next* to proceed.

Key in the information and please remember key as this key will be asked every time before the computer boots to Ubuntu.

After keying in the information, click **Next** to proceed with the installation as the process will be the same as default installation.

MANUAL PARTITION

Please be cautious as this step will affect your partitionin process.

As before, on Type of Installation have two options which **_Erase disk and install Ubuntu_** and **_Manual partitioning_**.

In **_Manual partitioning_** will have more options in creating partitioning.

Select **_Manual partitioning_** and click **_Next_**.

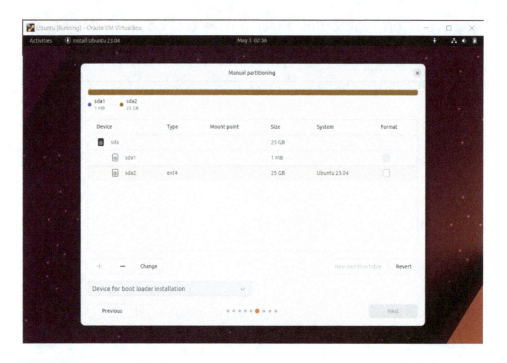

Showing the information regarding the disk information in graphic. Click **Change** to start modified partitioning.

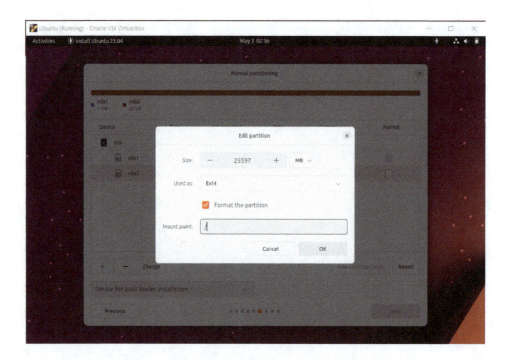

Change the size to the maximum size available then choose **Ext4** as partition format. Check the **Format the partition**, for the mount point type **/** then click **OK**.

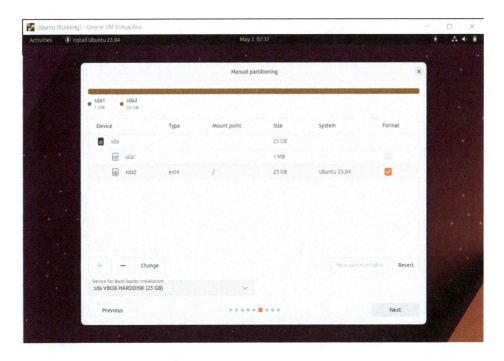

Changes already shown, if any changes need to be modified, may change as required. Click **Next** to proceed with the installation.

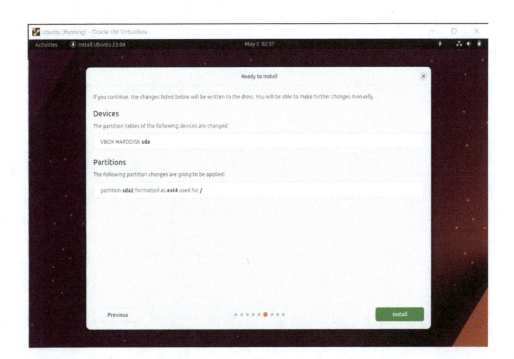

The screen showing the information, click **Previous** if need to change if confirm the action, click **Install**.

ACTIVE DIRECTORY

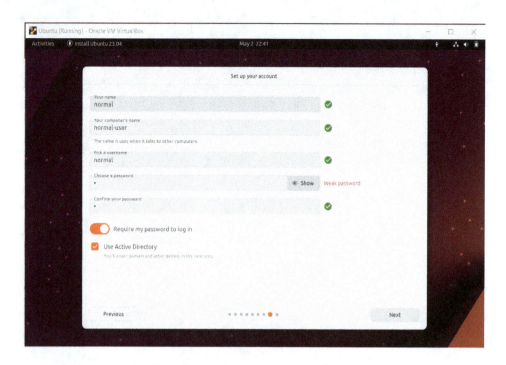

Check *Use Active Directory* then click *Next.*

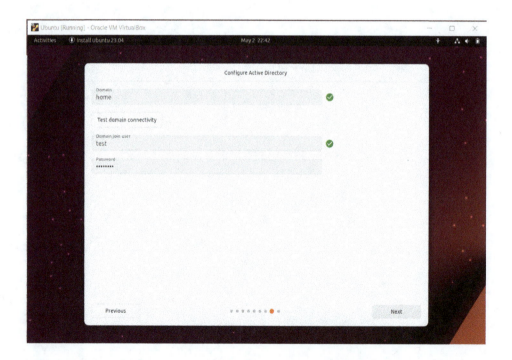

Fill in the information for the *Domain*, *Domain join user* and *password* as provided by Account Administrator. Click *Test domain connectivity* to test the setting and click Next to continue.

Active Directory needs a valid user account, password, and domain to connect to as the user will be verified by the Active Directory Server before allowing access.

LEGACY DESKTOP INSTALLER.

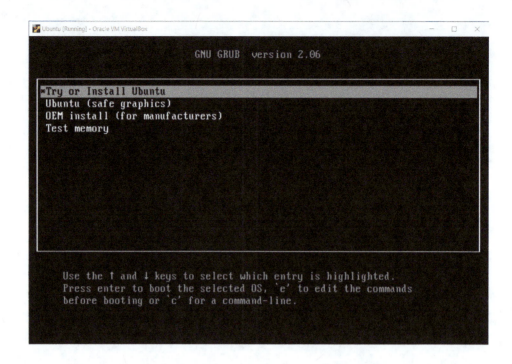

To start the installation, select **_Try or Install Ubuntu_** to proceed.

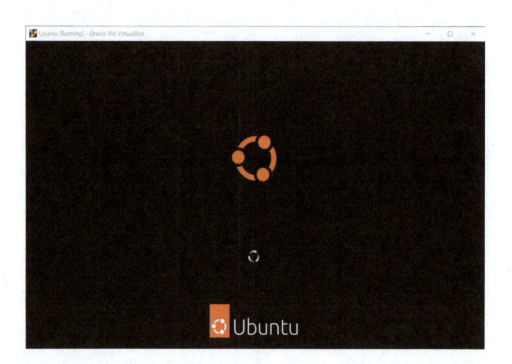

Ubuntu will be loaded into the computer, but no installation is being made.

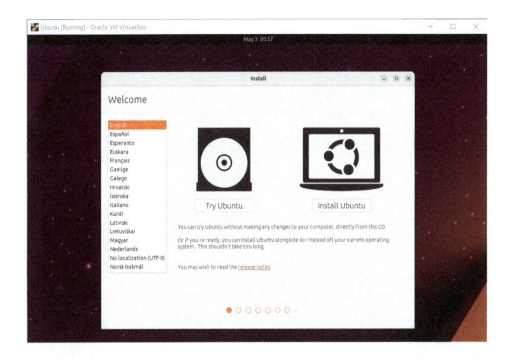

A window will appear, showing a few options such as the language wanted to be used during installation. Click **_Install Ubuntu_** to proceed with the installation.

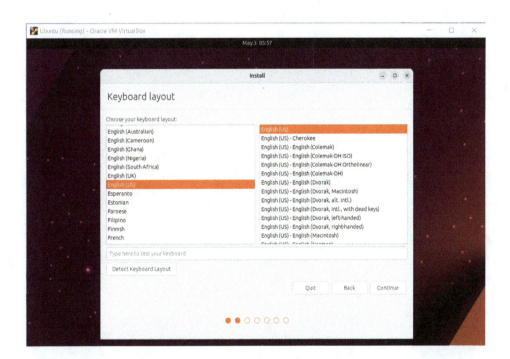

Choose the keyboard layout or click **_Detect Keyboard Layout_** for Ubuntu to detect automatically. Then click **_Continue_** to proceed.

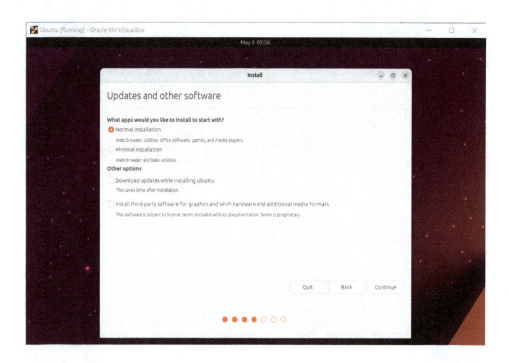

Select **Normal Installation** for the suggested application software to be installed.

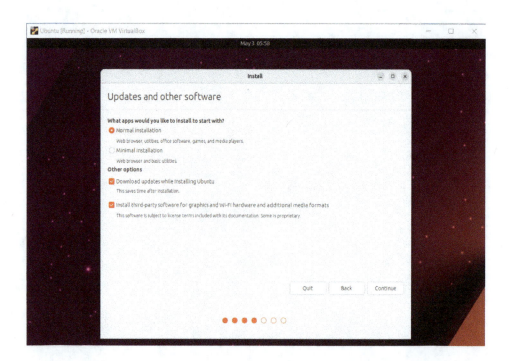

Select also option **Download update while installing ubuntu** to install updated packages during installation and **Install third-party software for graphic and Wi-Fi hardware and additional media format**s.

Then click **Continue**

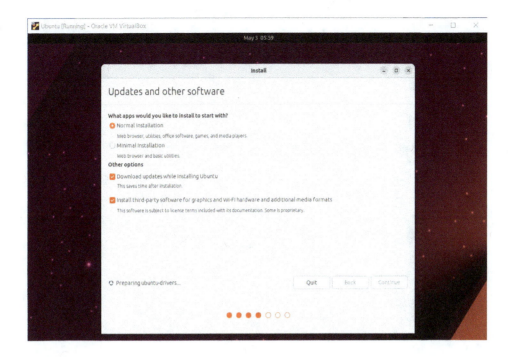

This will be preparing ubuntu driver before continuing to next step.

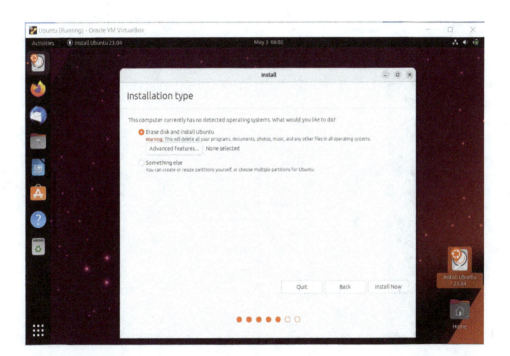

Choose *Erase disk and Install Ubuntu.*

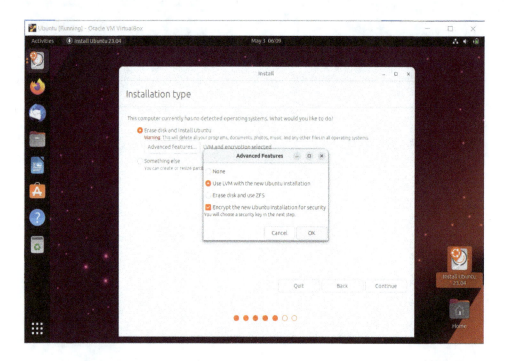

Option Use *LVM with new Ubuntu installation* or *Erase disk and use ZFS*. Choose either one.

Select *Encrypt the new Ubuntu installation for security* for more secure system.

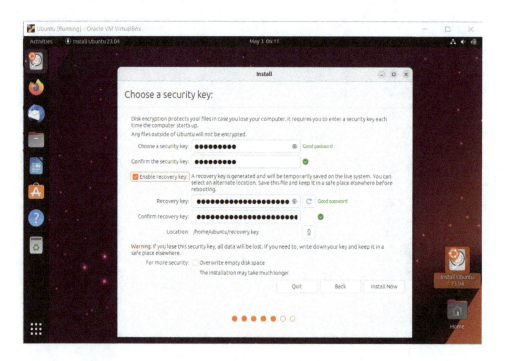

Key-in the security key information and remember the information as this key is required before booting into Ubuntu.

Also download the recovery key from the respected location as shown. May refer to page 89 for futher information.

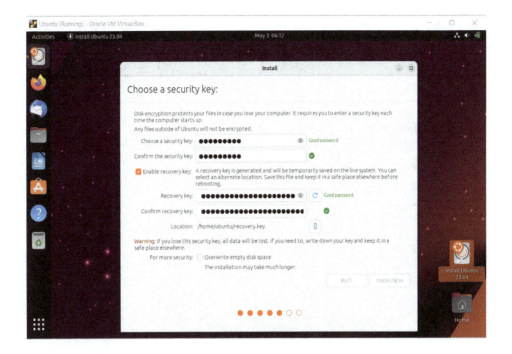

Click **Install Now** to proceed.

On screen Installation type, if choose **Something else** there is another step need to be taken. Refer to next page.

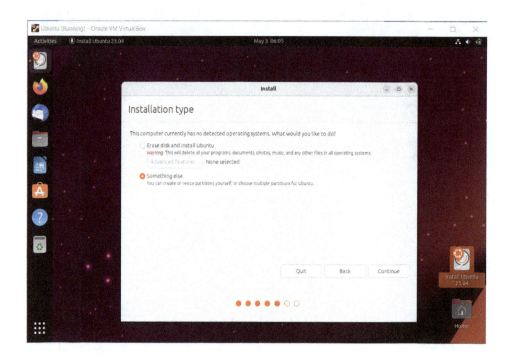

Select *Something else* then click *Continue*.

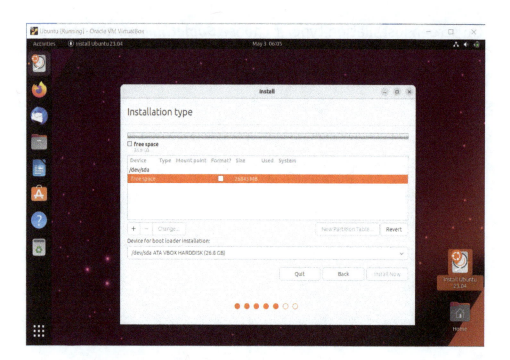

Click **+** to start creating the partition.

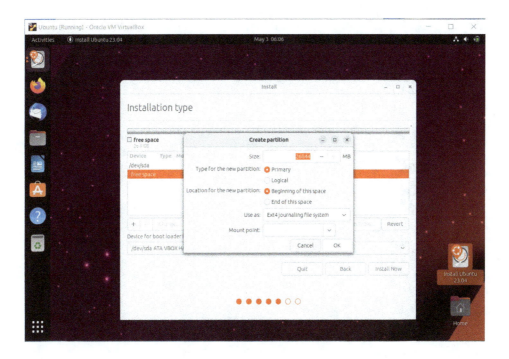

Use the maximum size allowed by the partition. Choose **Prima-ry** for the type for the new partition and select **Beginning** of this space for Location for new partition.

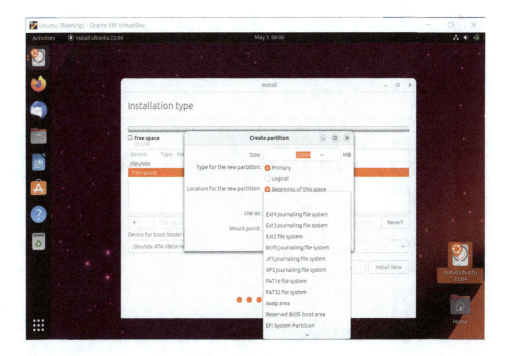

Click **Use as**, will list supported file system.

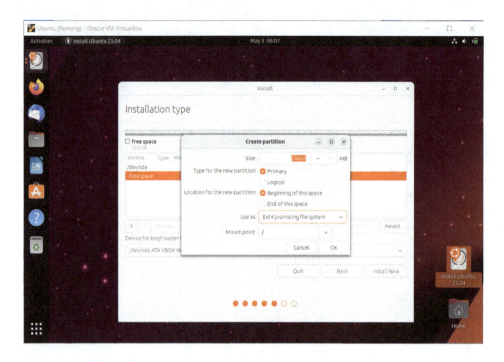

Choose **Ext4 journaling file system** and Mount point **/**.

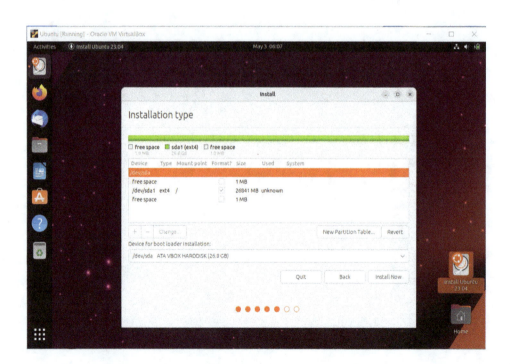

Information based on created previous configuration shown. Then click **Install Now** to proceed.

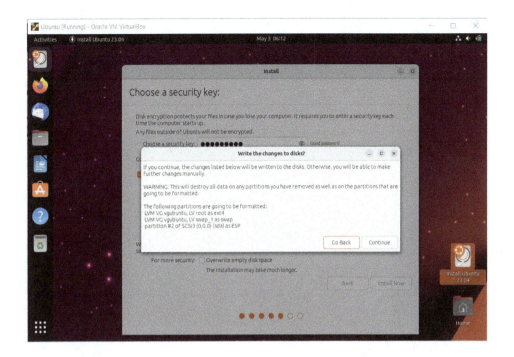

Changes will be written when click **Continue**, if need modification click the **Go Back** button.

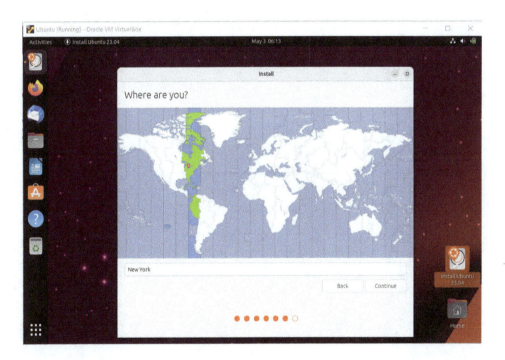

Click on your current location on the maps. Click **Next** to proceed.

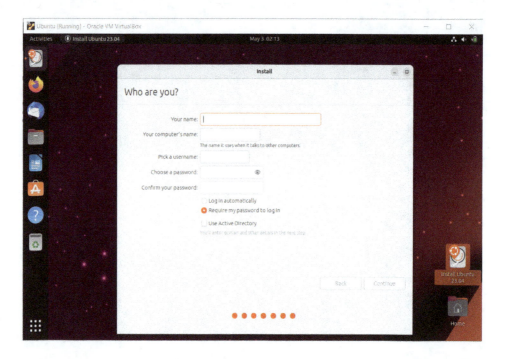

Fill in the information required and make sure to use a strong password to secure the account. If using a not secure password, notification Weak Password will show beside the password field.

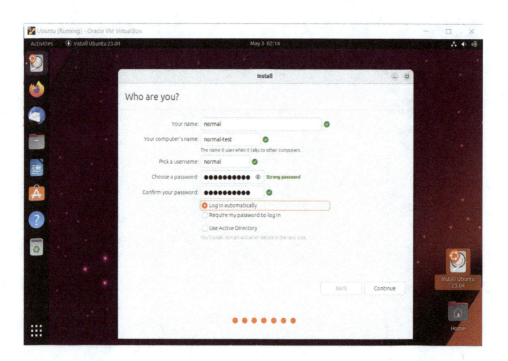

Strong Password notification appears if the password meets the security requirement. Select the Required my password to log in to make sure the user log into the system has the right privilege.

Click **Continue** to proceed.

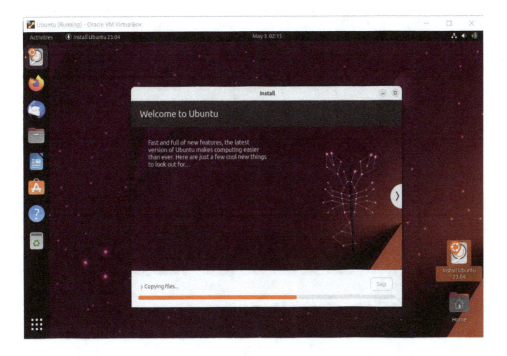

This screen is the installation process, just leave as it until the process completed.

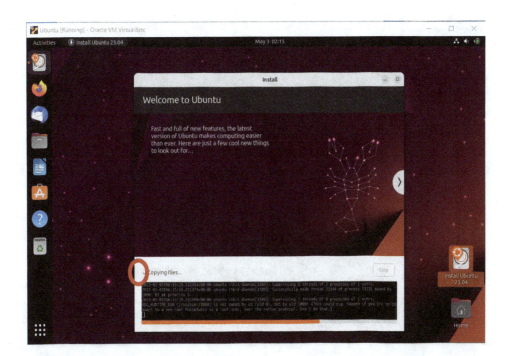

During the installation, if click item in red, will show the progress of installation.

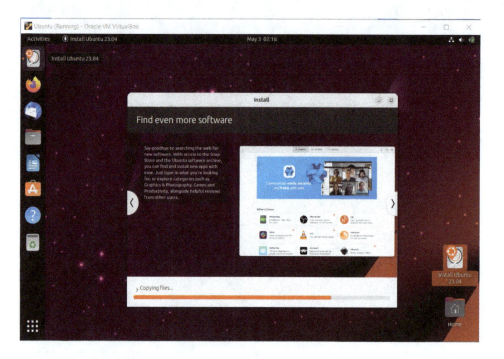

Showing the progress of the installation.

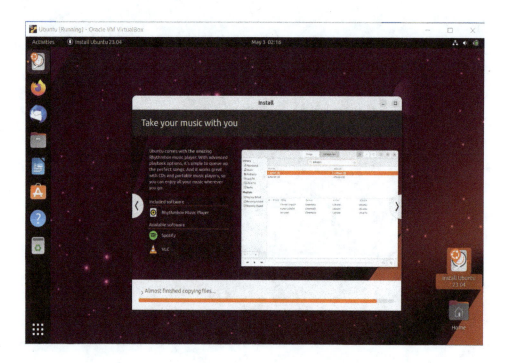

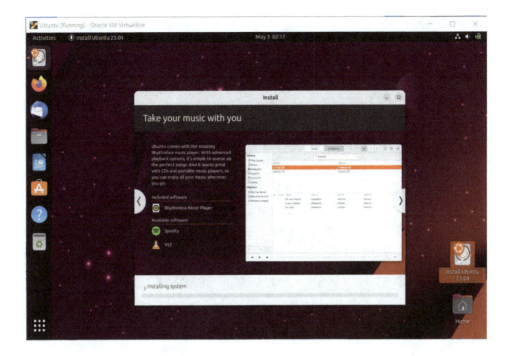

Showing the progress of the installation.

Showing the progress of the installation.

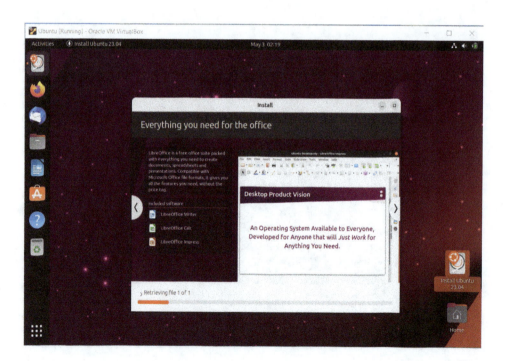

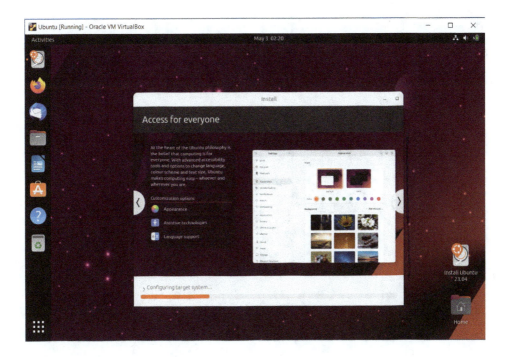

Showing the progress of the installation.

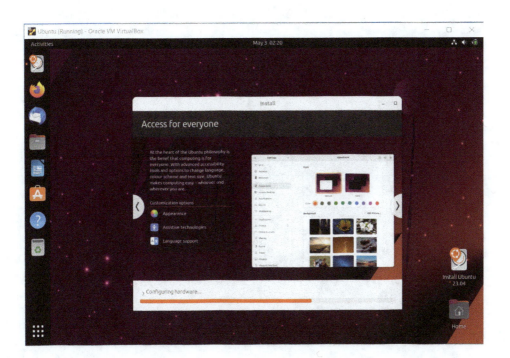

Showing the progress of the installation.

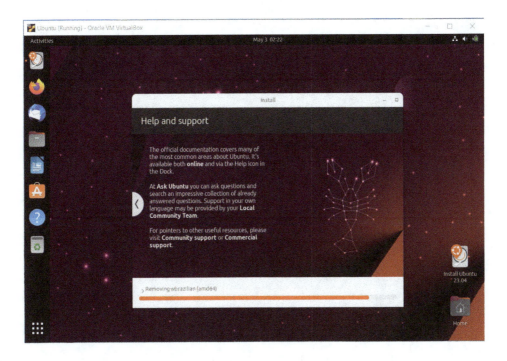

Showing the progress of the installation.

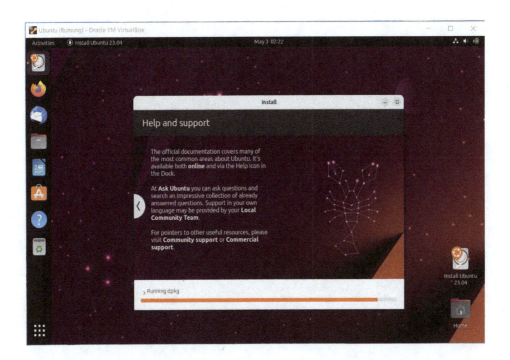

Showing the progress of the installation.

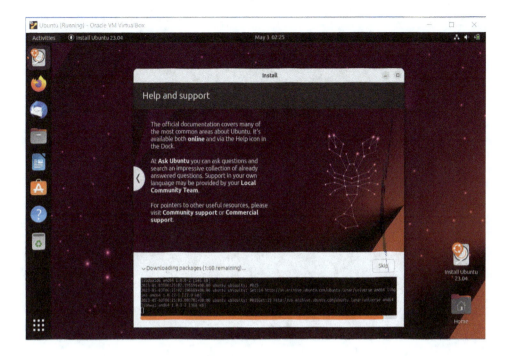

Showing the progress of the installation.

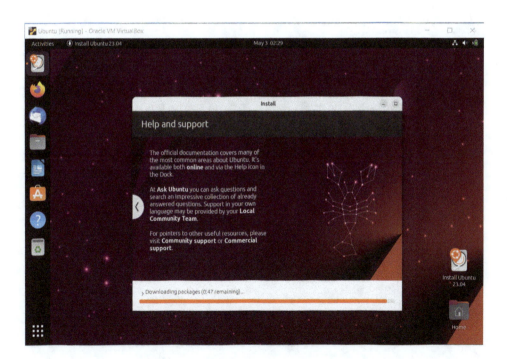

Showing the progress of the installation.

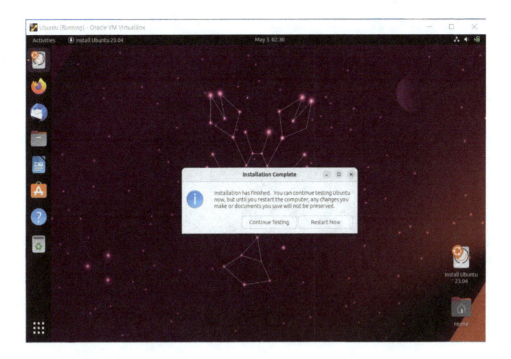

Click **Restart Now** to proceed.

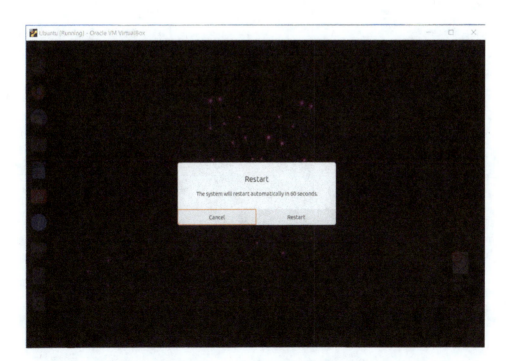

Notification appears before the restarting process.

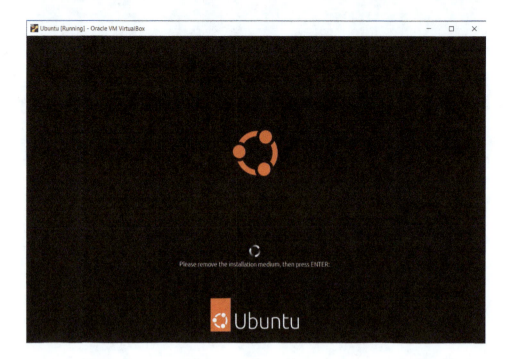

Remove the installation media. If using DVD or USB flash drive remove the drive, or using ISO unmount the media in the virtualization application.

After the media removal, the process rebooting will continue.

If previous use option **Encrypt the new Ubuntu installation**, this
screen will appear every time before booting to Ubuntu.

Cannot proceed without valid key provided before.

Key-in the credentials.

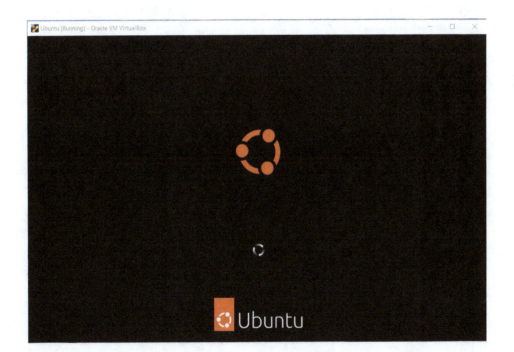

The process booting in progress.

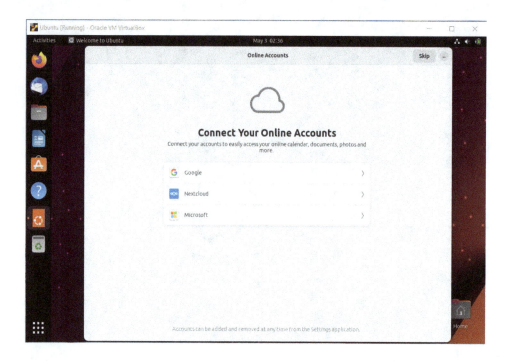

A window will show, to connect to Online Accounts or may proceed by clicking the **Skip** button on top right.

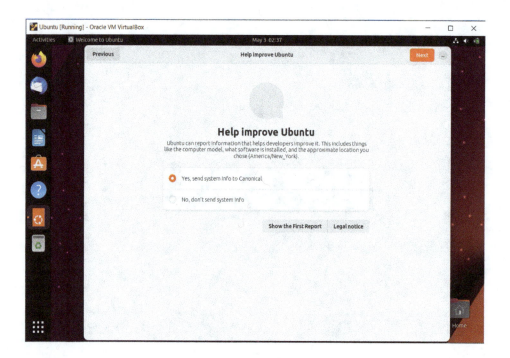

Option to share the information system, if agree to share select **Yes, send system info to Canonical** or disagrees select **No, don't send system info**. Then click **Next** to continue.

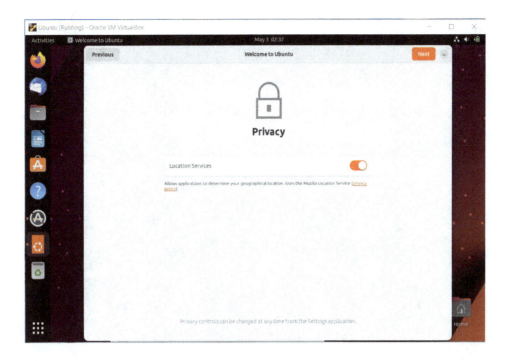

Location Services if enable will help to automatically detect the location of the computer. Click Next to proceed to the next step.

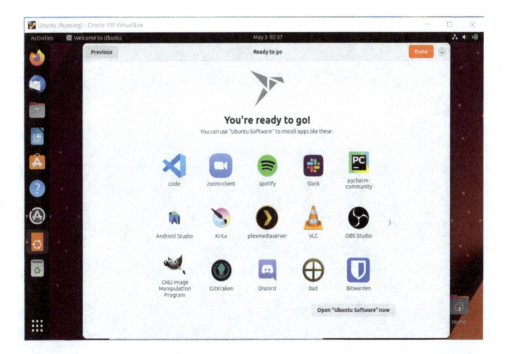

All the primary steps were completed. Click **Done** to end the process and if want to add/remove software may click Open Ubuntu Software.

If a new update is available, a window will appear showing the information about the update. Click Install Now if want to update.

Showing the update progress.

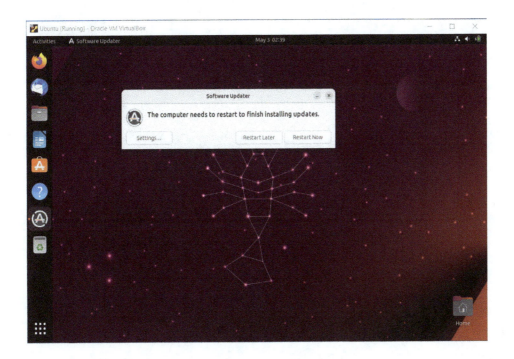

Showing the completed update progress.

For manual update refer page *81*

TERMINAL UPDATE

Updating package or application in Ubuntu can be done via terminal or using the Software application. Usually from time to time, the system will be checking the list of the files that need to be updated from the ubuntu repository. Any new update available, notification will prompt for update and proceed with the update.

The repository server can be change from the setting, please check with ubuntu official mirror list
https://launchpad.net/ubuntu/+archivemirrors.

Choose the nearest to your location as will speed up the update.

Mirror.johnnybegood.fr-archive	https http rsync	1 Gbps	Up to date
Ircam	http ftp rsync	1 Gbps	Up to date
Université de Nantes	http ftp rsync	1 Gbps	Up to date
LIP6/Sorbonne Université	https http ftp rsync	1 Gbps	Up to date
Université de Picardie	https http	100 Mbps	Up to date
CNRS/IPSL	http ftp rsync	45 Mbps	Up to date
Universite Reims Champagne-Ardenne	http ftp	10 Mbps	Up to date
Georgia		**1 Gbps**	**1 mirror**
GRENA	http	1 Gbps	Up to date
Germany		**232 Gbps**	**44 mirrors**
RWTH Aachen University	http ftp rsync	20 Gbps	Up to date
Uni Stuttgart	https http ftp rsync	20 Gbps	Up to date
dogado GmbH	https http rsync	20 Gbps	Up to date
NetCologne	https http ftp rsync	20 Gbps	Up to date
LRZ	http rsync	20 Gbps	Up to date
Clouvider	https http	10 Gbps	Up to date
Charite Berlin	https http	10 Gbps	Up to date
ScutNet Bonn	http ftp rsync	10 Gbps	Up to date
23media	http rsync	10 Gbps	Up to date
creoline GmbH	https http rsync	10 Gbps	Up to date
LeaseWeb Germany GmbH	https http ftp rsync	10 Gbps	Up to date
IPB Internet Provider in Berlin GmbH	http rsync	10 Gbps	Up to date
wilhelm.tel GmbH	http	10 Gbps	Up to date
xTom	https http rsync	10 Gbps	Up to date
Technische Universität Dresden	http rsync	10 Gbps	Up to date
Friedrich-Alexander-Universität Erlangen-Nürnberg	http ftp rsync	4 Gbps	Up to date
Esslingen University of Applied Sciences	http ftp rsync	2 Gbps	Up to date
University of Kaiserslautern	http ftp rsync	2 Gbps	Up to date

Washington State University	http	100 Mbps	Up to date
Secured Servers LLC	http	100 Mbps	Up to date
University of West Georgia	http rsync	45 Mbps	Up to date
Indiana University	http	10 Mbps	Up to date
Virginia Commonwealth University	http ftp	10 Mbps	Up to date
Uruguay		**145 Mbps**	**2 mirrors**
Universidad de la República	http	100 Mbps	Up to date
UDELAR-CURE	https http	45 Mbps	Up to date
Uzbekistan		**100 Mbps**	**1 mirror**
ISP Sarkor Telecom	http ftp	100 Mbps	Up to date
Viet Nam		**3 Gbps**	**7 mirrors**
BizFly Cloud	http	1 Gbps	Last update unknown
Vietnix	http	1 Gbps	Up to date
BKNS.VN	https http rsync	1 Gbps	Up to date
clearsky.vn	http	100 Mbps	Up to date
Nhan Hoa	http	100 Mbps	Up to date
eHost	http	100 Mbps	Up to date
XTDV Group	http	100 Mbps	Up to date
Total			
		2984 Gbps	**574 mirrors**

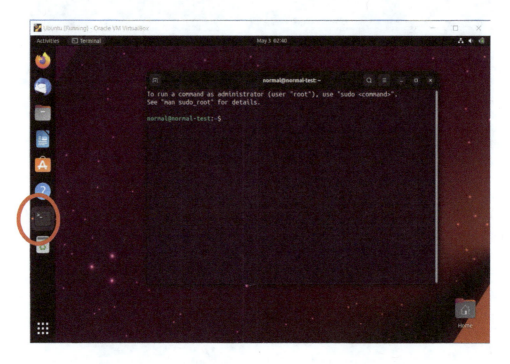

On the left side, click the icon in red color, this will open terminal application.

On the terminal application, type

sudo apt update

Key-in the credential or password created before. The key-in character won't be displayed as part of the security.

If wrong credentials or password given, this error will appear.

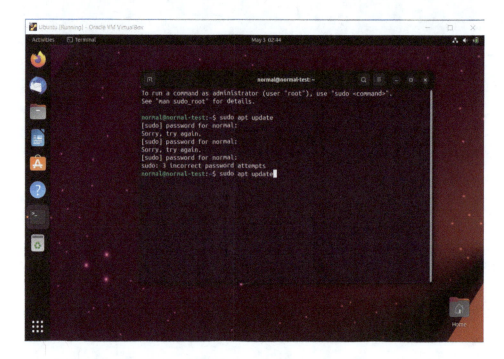

Again, on the terminal application, type

sudo apt update

Progress getting the list of applications information.

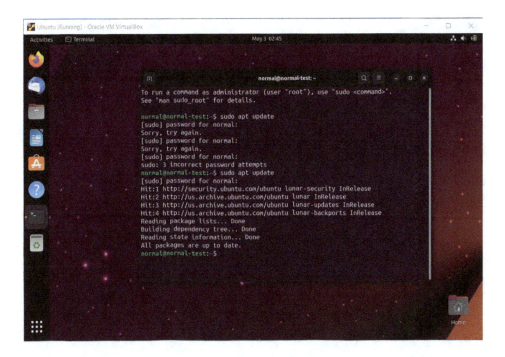

If all the applications have the latest updates, this reply will be

All packages are up to date

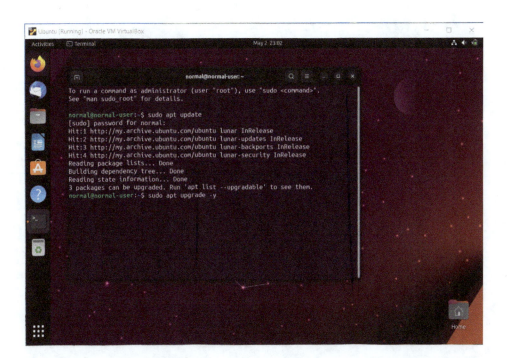

If available the application upgrade as shown, to upgrade the package type.

Sudo apt upgrade -y

This will retrieve the updated application packages from the server repository. The progress will show in the terminal.

After the updating the package done, the terminal will be release for next command to run.

CERT KEY

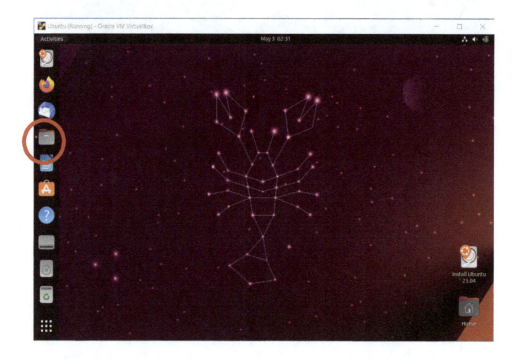

On left, click red circle application, will open Files Application as this will showing all available files.

Copy the *recovery.key* to another storage device or may attach the key via email.

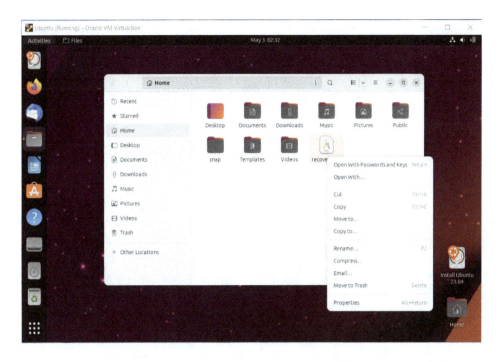

Right click, to see the available option. As the key is very important, please save the file as if lost, no recovery can be done.

END

www.ingramcontent.com/pod-product-compliance
Lightning Source LLC
LaVergne TN
LVHW081700050326
832903LV00026B/1850